MICHAEL GILLETTE

Collecting Stamps

A hobby that can last a lifetime! You can collect stamps on your own or you can invite your family and friends to join you in this wonderful world of stamps!

Copyright © 2024 by Michael Gillette

All rights reserved. No part of this publication may be reproduced, stored or transmitted in any form or by any means, electronic, mechanical, photocopying, recording, scanning, or otherwise without written permission from the publisher. It is illegal to copy this book, post it to a website, or distribute it by any other means without permission.

Michael Gillette asserts the moral right to be identified as the author of this work.

Michael Gillette has no responsibility for the persistence or accuracy of URLs for external or third-party Internet Websites referred to in this publication and does not guarantee that any content on such Websites is, or will remain, accurate or appropriate.

Designations used by companies to distinguish their products are often claimed as trademarks. All brand names and product names used in this book and on its cover are trade names, service marks, trademarks and registered trademarks of their respective owners. The publishers and the book are not associated with any product or vendor mentioned in this book. None of the companies referenced within the book have endorsed the book.

First edition

This book was professionally typeset on Reedsy.
Find out more at reedsy.com

Contents

	Prologue	1
	Introduction	2
1	Chapter 1	3
2	Chapter 2	6
3	Chapter 3	10
4	Chapter 4	17
5	Chapter 5	21
6	Conclusion	24
	Afterword	26

Prologue

I promise to see and hear all the wonderful people that enrich my life, family and friends and to be sincerely thankful for all of them, often and unconditionally.

Introduction

On a quiet day, have you ever said to yourself, or even out loud to someone nearby "I'm bored!" Or "there is nothing for me to do!" This book has an answer to that problem. The purpose of this book is to show you that you can have something to do no matter when or where you are today. The answer is collecting stamps. You may have heard and thought about stamp collecting at some point and you've been curious about the hobby but were not sure that the hobby is for you. With collecting stamps, you are looking into a wonderful hobby that can be very satisfying. All it takes is a little imagination.

Chapter 1

Collecting Stamps

The hobby of Collecting Stamps has a formal name. That name is philately. It is a hobby that has enchanted young and old people for many generations. President Franklin Roosevelt was an avid collector of stamps, there are many stories and photographs of him enjoying his collection. Collecting Stamps involves gathering several stamp related items including postage stamps, postmarks, postcards, hunting permit stamps, savings stamps, and many other stamp related items. Collecting stamps is indeed a hobby that can provide a glimpse into the rich history and cultures of all the countries of the world over hundreds of years but stamps also can offer a unique way to appreciate art, design, and geography. From rare and valuable stamps to modern stamps sold every day there is something in the hobby for everyone.

The Character of Stamps

Collecting stamps has something for everyone, whether you are a curious novice thinking about starting your first stamp collection or an experienced collector seeking to expand your treasure trove. Let's rummage through the fascinating hobby for a moment and explore the ways stamps can help us learn about history, and some of the many ways stamp collectors make their hobby one that can last a lifetime.

As you begin your own journey into collecting stamps you will hear a lot about rare and valuable stamps, and modern stamps, as well as stamps sold every day. There are some things to keep in the back of your mind about those stamp descriptions. According to the United States Postal Service "13.68 Billion postage stamps were printed in 2023. United States postage stamps are miniature works of art designed to reflect the American experience. Stamps highlight heroes, history, milestones, achievements and natural wonders."

Now, considering that the United States printed over 13 Billion postage stamps in 2023, and all the other countries of the world likely printed billions combined, what would be the factors that make a stamp rare today? Some factors for modern stamp rarity (year 1940 to present day) would be printing errors including the colors misaligned, an item on the stamp printed in the wrong place or even upside down or sideways. A color mismatched or a color missing and letters or words missing. These are just a few identifiable mistakes; the list could be as long as any kind of manufacturing mistake could occur.

Other conditions that could cause a stamp to be considered rare can include the number of stamps printed of one type, and the estimated amount that remain in existence today.

Surprisingly, the rarer the stamp, the likelihood that the ownership and whereabouts of most known copies are identified and recorded today.The Inverted Jenny stamp is a well-known example of a very rare error stamp. The Jenny stamp is a $.24 cent Airmail stamp printed in 1918. It involved one sheet of 100 stamps. The stamp consisted of a red border and a blue biplane. The biplane was mistakenly printed upside-down on each of the 100 stamps. Recently one Inverted Jenny stamp sold at an auction for $2,000,000.00 (2 million dollars.)

The inverted Jenny is an example of a Classic era stamp.Classic Era

CHAPTER 1

stamps were created between 1840 to 1940. There are many examples of earlier provincial stamps having been created by local post offices worldwide. They were easily counterfeited and not organized well at all. On May 6, 1840, Great Britain began selling a stamp commonly called the "Penny Black". The Penny Black Stamp, despite its history and age, is not considered a rare stamp. According to Stanley Gibbons.com "there were over 68 million Penny Black Stamps printed, and it is estimated that approximately 5% still survive. Nevertheless, depending on circumstances, some of them can be very valuable with the rarest pieces changing hands well more than £100,000."

2

Chapter 2

The Beauty of Stamps

Every stamp regardless of its country of origin is truly a work of art. The adhesive stamps issued today by the United States Postal Service (USPS) are colorful and precise depictions of the items they represent. Earlier stamps were engraved and the figures and items they represent were created with great detail; many were engraved in the same manner that United States Currency was created. Each stamp regardless of what era, year or decade from which they originate are undeniably beautiful. We will get more into the beauty of stamps soon.

The History and Nostalgia of Collecting Stamps

Collections of any kind take on the personality of what the collector wants their collection to represent. Early on the stamp collector will consider if the collection will be open and inviting to anyone, or held privately, solely for the collector's enjoyment. It's safe to say that anything can be collected. Stamps are uniquely positioned for that as there are many, many ways to collect stamps. If you enjoy historic moments in time, or places, or events, stamps have something for you. If you like outer space, motor vehicles of all kinds, animals, geographic locations, famous people, trees, flowers, airplanes and air travel, war events and people who fought them, Presidents and other World Leaders and Statesmen, Holidays, Comic characters, celebrities, Schools and learning, again stamps really do have something for you. If you are interested in another country and the stamps issued there, you will find exciting things there too.

The Wonder of Collecting Stamps

The next time you receive an envelope that has a postage stamp affixed to it, try to sit down, slow down for just a moment and really look at that stamp. It doesn't matter what stamp it is, really look at it. Ask yourself, what is the stamp showing you? Is it a picture of flowers? What are the colors, do you know what the name of the flower is? Do you know where that flower can grow?

Could the stamp be a patriotic symbol and some stylized rendition of our country's flag? Do you know if the symbol has a specific meaning to its design? After looking and thinking about that picture, how did it make you feel?

Perhaps the stamp was a picture of the birth of Christ, or maybe of a menorah, or a picture of an apple or some other fruit like an orange.It could be a picture of a Muscle Car from the 1970's that sparks your interest and sets in motion some recent memory of seeing a model of that car at a neighborhood car show and it helps you remember an enjoyable time with people you were there with. It could be a memory of current friends, or it could be a fond memory of parents, grandparents or other important people from our past. The treasure here is that you can pause, look at the picture and think of what the stamp represents and oftentimes the stamp will tell you, just by the picture enough information is there to let you travel to that item, location or time and be able to sense the story the stamp is so eloquently broadcasting.

During the early 1940's the world was full of stamps depicting war propaganda. Both Allied and Axis used postage stamps to attract stamp collectors and used their stamps to tell their story of strength and the will to win the war, and further tell of tragedy and victories to raise awareness and money to fund the war effort. If you have a chance to view those stamps in person or just in a catalog of world stamps it will be a worthwhile exploration. Further, if you allow yourself to let your mind travel back to see the events, people and places the stamps represent, You'll see the world as most people today have never seen it. The level of care put into creating most of those stamps is truly impressive, how the stamps show the will, the strife and suffering and victories of people is immense. The subject matter, while very important, is your decision to make it relevant within your own perspective.

Different Ways to Collect Stamps

This book is, as mentioned, intended to help a curious person consider taking up collecting stamps. Here is a list of just a few ways to collect stamps.

If you are artistic, you can make an album page of a stamp incorporated within a color pencil drawing or watercolor that you've made of the stamp itself.

You can collect single stamps, sets of two adjoining stamps, four adjoining stamps in a row, or square.

Stamps on envelopes, or stamps cut off the envelope but with the post mark still attached.

Stamps can be easily collected without spending a lot of money by looking at your own mail and cutting off the postmark and stamp(s) and temporarily storing them in a plain old shoe box.

If you explain your intentions to collect stamps and ask friends, family members, neighbors and if possible, anywhere else that you might think of that receives mail to save their empty envelopes with stamps attached for you. You might be surprised at their eagerness to help you build your collection. Some might even give you a dusty old forgotten stamp album that's been stored in their attic from their past that they are excited to pass on to you. Try to remember that the stamps you collect and save from the garbage dumpster today will have a very good chance of being that 100-year-old stamp in a collection belonging to someone dear to you someday.

As time passes your collection will become more important to you and you will want to take better care of them. There are several ways to take care of and display your collection. You can take these steps gradually, though in time as your collection grows you will want to take these steps. I'll go further and encourage you to take very good care of your stamps. You'll want them to last a very long time. The only way to help them age well is to take steps to make that happen.

Chapter 3

Out of the Shoe box

1. The important tools needed to start a collection and tools for future growth of your collection as well as how to protect, store and display your stamps
2. Good Old Shoe Boxes
3. Glassine Envelopes
4. A Stamp Album
5. Mounting Materials
6. Gloves, Tongs, Magnifying Glasses

Shoe Boxes are fine when you first start watching your mail and collecting those stamps and if your collection grows, you'll need boxes to store your tools, stamp care materials and extra stamps.

Glassine Envelopes are important for your stamp collection. Glassine envelopes help protect your stamps from moisture, dirt and unnecessary handling. Glassine envelopes come in many sizes and are not expensive and are worth having. When you buy stamps at the post office, ask the Postal Clerk to put the stamps in a glassine envelope. Even if that stamp

CHAPTER 3

purchase isn't intended to be part of your collection you will have a glassine envelope to use for your collection. Glassine envelopes are used to not only protect your collection from contaminants, but they are also used to store your stamps, especially duplicate stamps. The envelopes are easy to see in and can help you to store your stamps in an order of your choosing without having to always open and remove the contents to see what is in the envelope.

Cataloging Your Collection

The Scott Catalog produced by the Amos Media Company prints a series of catalogs that are updated annually. Every stamp possibly released from most every country has been cataloged and given a "Scott Catalog Number". It is those Scott catalog numbers that your stamp collection can be filed by. Using the Scott number is beneficial because the numbers are universally recognized and if you mention a number to another collector, they can easily research which stamp you are talking about. An example of a Scott Catalog number is C3a, remember the Inverted Jenny Stamp? C3a is Jenny's Scott Catalog Number! At the time of this writing, the most recent Scott catalog stamp number is Scott 7X2, which is for a 5¢ black Millbury, Mass., postmaster's provisional stamp on white print paper. This stamp was discovered in 2024 and logged into the Scott United States Specialized catalog. The most recent United States Postal Service regular mail Ansel Adams pane of 16 stamps has been assigned the Scott number 5854 A through P. Another advantage of the Scott Catalog is that along with a handy universal identification number, the catalog also provides a good estimate of what your stamp could be worth depending upon the condition of your stamp and often a good but brief description of the stamp including when and where it was issued.

Your Stamp Album

The next thing to consider is truly a gateway to be creative with your collection. It's in your stamp album where you will really decide what you want to collect and how you will choose to display the collection. Stamp albums help you to keep track of what your collection might be worth, and the album helps you identify what stamps in order of the stamp release that you are missing if you are inclined to collect stamps in that order. There are several commercial albums that you can buy. Commercial Albums offer predetermined album designs made to display your stamps in that predetermined order and theme.

An important point to consider when creating an album is that acid free paper is a must. Acid free paper protects your stamps from cross contamination with the paper which can create a chemical reaction and ruin the stamp by bleeding the acid used in paper manufacturing. If you have ever seen a newspaper after it has sat on a driveway in the sun for a few hours, you will understand what paper with an acid content looks like as it ages. Store bought stamp albums are made with acid free paper.

Mounting Tools and Materials

Stamp Tongs

Stamp Tongs are simply tweezers made specifically for use with your stamp collection. Stamp Collection Tongs are usually 4 to 6 inches long, longer tongs can be obtained if desired and the tips of the tongs are most always flat and thin rather than sharp and pointed. Tongs are important because they allow a collector to pick up and work with your stamps without using your hands or fingers which will leave body oil on the stamps that may not be visible for a long time but most assuredly will be there to ruin the stamp in most cases.

Watermarks

Some stamps are protected by watermarks. According to the Mystic Stamp Company, "stamp watermarks were introduced in 1895 as a way to deter counterfeiting. Most US stamps issued from that year to 1917 were printed on watermarked paper, with the very last being in 1938.

Watermarks consist of translucent impressions which allow more light to travel through the paper in the affected areas. This design was created by pressing a molded wire form (called a dandy roll) into wet paper pulp before the stamps were printed. For United States Stamps, only two watermarks were ever used: "USPS" (printed in double-line Capital Letters repeatedly across the back of the large sheet of stamp paper.) from 1895 onward and single-line (Bold Capital Letters) beginning in 1910 ending in 1938 was used.

Some Great Britain stamps picture watermarks in the shape of crowns while some stamps of India picture elephant watermarks. Other countries have interesting and unusual symbols in their watermarks, too.

Many people enjoy collecting watermarked stamps - it's like going on a treasure hunt!"

Detecting Watermarks

Not only are watermarks fun to see on a stamp, but the watermarks can also help you to discover stamp forgeries when buying a stamp and help determine which stamp variety you're dealing with. In several circumstances the Postal Service didn't watermark every stamp in a series, and early on, some stamp series were used by the Post Office for years, therefore earlier stamps may look the same on the face and have no watermark, but later stamps of the same series carried a watermark.

There are some methods that you can use to detect or see a watermark on a stamp. If you hold the stamp up to a bright light, you might be able to see the watermark. The best way to see if your stamp has a watermark is to use Watermark fluid. Clarity Watermark Fluid Catalog #LS115 is a very good choice of watermark fluid. It is made by the Mystic Stamp Company and is non-toxic unlike other petroleum products and provides excellent results. To detect the watermark: in a very small container pour in an equally small amount of fluid, just enough to cover a postage stamp. Put the stamp in the fluid first face down. Very soon after you should see the watermark start to appear. It will look slightly darker than the white paper around it. Keep in mind that United States Stamps will not show the entire "USPS" watermark on one stamp. You'll only see parts of one or two letters.

Magnifying Glass

A magnifying glass simply lets the viewer see intricate details on a stamp more clearly. There is no specific magnifying glass you should purchase. As your interest grows, you'll find that there are indeed specialized magnifiers to use to help with indexing a particular point on a stamp and easily show it to a friend or associate with little effort. These magnifiers have a thin line that can be dialed around a stamp so the line can mark and draw the viewer quickly to the topic point on the stamp of discussion.

Perforation Gauges

Many stamps look the same but are manufactured with different amounts of perforations on the sides of the stamps. For example, Booklet stamps, Coil Stamps, Sheet stamps all may look alike and yet have different perforation counts. All of these stamps are assigned their own catalog number. To determine which, stamp you are attempting to identify an accurate perforation count may be necessary. An easy way to make an accurate perforation count can be achieved by using a perforation gauge. The gauge usually has up to 16 different examples of perforations that are used by lining up the perforations on the stamp with the same outline on the gauge to see if you have a match. If not a match, you will eventually find it through trial and error by moving the gauge along the stamp until you find the match. Usually, you will know the range of perforations you are working in; therefore, it isn't always just a guessing game. These gauges are not expensive but can be a valuable addition to your stamp toolbox.

Stamp Hinges

Stamp hinges are a stamp collecting tool that has few if any similar competitors. Stamp hinges are used to attach your stamps to an album page. They act just like a door hinge when attached correctly to the stamp and album page. Hinges are made from glassine type acid free paper and have an adhesive side. They are sold, usually pre-folded in packs of 1000, 3000, and 5000 pieces. They cost about $4.00 for a package of 1000. Don't buy more than you need.They last a very long time but the cost warrants keeping a fresh supply on hand rather than so many that you will never use them all.

Hinges work by attaching the small part of the folding hinge by wetting the adhesive and affixing it very close to the top of the stamp, then affixing the longer back portion of the hinge to the album page. Attaching the stamp in this manner will allow you to lift the stamp to inspect the back of the stamp. Be sure that you want to use a hinge to affix the stamp to an album page. Later on, in the future if you want to move, sell or trade the stamp, the hinge will very likely leave a mark on the back of the stamp that will be detrimental to any potential value.

Stamp Mounts

Stamp mounts are a very good option for displaying your stamps and can be purchased in packages of 50 that are sized exactly for the size of the stamp you want to affix to your album page. Stamp Mounts surround your stamp with acid free plastic with usually black or white acid free paper backing. They can be purchased with adhesive backings or without adhesive. Mounts are good tools for storing your favorite stamps or stamps you might have paid a higher price to obtain. By storing your stamps in stamp mounts you have greater assurance from handling damage.

Color Guides

Color Guides are like a paint color palette you might see at a paint or hardware store with many small rectangles of multiple color samples attached in a corner to a ring. Postage Stamp Color Guides are exactly like that except they have the colors that make up stamps. Some stamps might have the same design, many classic and early modern era stamps do, and they are usually made in different colors for each denomination.

Some same denomination stamps might have a slightly different but distinct color. For example, red and crimson. The color gauge is just another way to help identify the stamp that you have.

4

Chapter 4

Where To Go For More Information About Collecting Stamps

Local Stamp Collector Clubs

One of the most rewarding things about a hobby is being able to share it with other people. Especially like-minded people. If you are still curious about collecting stamps, try to find a local stamp collectors club. There are many advantages to being a member of a local club. You can ask questions from experienced collectors. As time goes by you will find yourself answering questions those individuals may ask of you. Either way all the club members, in small or large groups, will gladly welcome you. Some members may help you identify local resources to find stamps, they may even share a handful of the duplicates they have at home in their own faithful old shoe box.

Regional Stamp Shows

Seek out regional stamp shows that may be held within traveling distance for you. Stamp shows involve several opportunities. One of my favorites is if the show is big enough, the United States Postal Service may schedule a Postage Stamp launch at the show. A Postage Stamp launch involves the release of a brand new, never offered for sale stamp. Along with the launch the Local Post Office will usually have a sales booth where a customer can purchase several items related to the new stamp, including but not limited to a First Day Cover! First day covers are envelopes. Cover was a term used a long time ago before formal envelopes like we have today were manufactured. The "cover" covered the letter. Before that, the letter was folded in any number of ways to allow the recipient the ability to know if the letter was read in transit by someone other than the addressee.

First Day Covers are special to some collectors because they bear a postmark displaying the date the stamp was issued along with a banner in the postmark stating this is a FIRST DAY OF ISSUE and usually the location of the issue. Often on site some supply companies and private vendors will sell envelopes with an artistic version of the stamp drawn or painted on the "cover". You then purchase the stamp, attach it to the cover and the postal worker will cancel the stamp with the First Day of Issue cancellation thereby making your souvenir a real limited-edition treasure.

Another way to acquire a first day of issue cancellation is to research when and where a stamp will be issued. Learn what United States Post Office is scheduled to oversee the first day issue. You can put a self-addressed envelope with a personal check or money order for the amount of the stamp being released in a larger envelope with a letter to the Postmaster asking that the envelope be affixed with the first day stamp the day of the first issue with the first day cancellation. The Postmaster will gladly help with your request. However, an easier and more efficient way to get your First Day Covers is to go here: https://store.usps.com/store/results?tt=First+Day+of+Issue&_requestid=5060777

Hobby Stores

Big box hobby stores are great for finding supplies and even packets of used stamps that you'll find fun to add to your collection. Yet, small local hobby shops that usually deal in collections like Stamps, Coins, and Baseball cards are great resources to talk about and obtain supplies and of course stamps. Just catch them when they aren't too busy to talk to you.

Your Workplace

Your place of work is an exceptional place to talk about your stamp collecting hobby. You'll find that over time coworkers will begin to share their experiences with stamp collecting. Some coworkers may have old stamps in their attics they no longer want and may give them to you or offer the collection to you at incredible discounts. Some may tell you about an old collection they have had in their closet for a long time and now that you brought it up may be thinking about selling it. They may even ask you to look at the collection and give them an idea of what it might be worth. In that instance, if you have a catalog, be willing to sit down with them and go through their album or shoebox to help them learn about their stamps. You can do the same online. Often on-line auctions will give you better pricing examples than just looking in the catalog. Be sure you know the principles of grading stamps before attempting to suggest a value on a stamp. In the end be as honest as you possibly can. These are your friends. You never know when someone may have that diamond in the rough. It will come when you least expect it, for sure.

Schools

Schools can be a good place to share your stamp collecting hobby. If you are a student, a teacher or some other member of the school faculty, if there isn't an inter-school stamp club, ask through proper channels to start a Stamp Collectors Club. If permission is granted, seek to learn the formal nuances of operating a club in the school setting. Be sure to keep the meetings frequent, but not too frequent and most of all interesting.

5

Chapter 5

Stamp Collecting For A Lifetime, (And Not Just Yours!)

You've learned that collecting stamps gives us the opportunity to travel and learn about different countries, the people who live there and what they enjoy and what they are like, their heritage and their ancestors. The stamps let us travel by train, ride a horse and fly to the moon and back, defend your country, celebrate famous people and their inventions and most places and things in between.

However, some collectors save stamps for profit and the stories their stamps tell are a means to an end. If you buy and sell at a profit enough, even with the least expensive stamps, you are likely to make some money. While it's not likely that your collection will ever have a high monetary value, it is possible that you can strive for the one or two stamps that you would like to call your own that will have some monetary value whatever amount that means to you at any given moment.

Quite a while ago, around 1985, I was just starting to play with the idea of collecting stamps when a person very dear to me named Ruby said that she too started her own stamp collection a long time before that, approximately 1940. She explained that she no longer had the ability or desire to carry on with the collection and hadn't for quite some time.

She offered her collection to me at a reasonable exchange, and I gladly accepted the offer. Her collection was very extensive where the decade of the 1940's was concerned. She had a wonderful mix of deeper years and of newer years, in her collection she had older tools that she used to work on her collection, and it excited my imagination to no end. The fire for collecting she lit beneath me forty years ago is undeniable and genuine. I will forever be grateful for that wonderful act of caring she gave to me that summer.

Those old stamps that she had in her collection, some dating back even further than the 1940's in 1985, were 50 to maybe 75 or 80-years-old, none were worth much of anything, but they are 100 and some 110 years old in 2024! Those stamps and the many stamps, first day covers, old letters and postcards that I have bought at auctions, shows, stores and from friends as well as some that have been gifted to me by dear friends, for me, are a wonder just to hold. I can't explain the thrill and what it is like when I discovered a letter in an auction that was mailed a hundred years ago or more to or by people that lived in my hometown.

Ruby shared her collection that she held close for most of her lifetime. Rather than split it up and send it off to someone who would tear it down and sell it mostly piece by piece, she trusted me to keep it intact and grow the collection which I have done. Something that I will do someday when I find the right curious person that might keep it safe, grow it and pass it along to the next curious person. That is how a Stamp Collection can become a hobby of a lifetime. I can't help but wonder how many people would share this idea if they just recognized what joy that dusty old one-quarter filled stamp album could do to bring their family or friends today in such a busy era.

Keeping your hobby of collecting stamps going for a lifetime will become second nature for you at some point. One day you'll find yourself getting excited inside when someone mentions that they have this old stamp album in the closet, and they don't know anything about it. You

CHAPTER 5

will get excited to ask questions and ask to see it. You will also find yourself tearing the corners off every stamped envelope that you come across, making sure to tear off just enough so you can trim the excess paper around the postmark and the stamp. Sadly, most mail that comes to my mailbox today are nonprofits and advertisements, still if the envelope has a stamp, the stamp comes off! That is a reason to seek out someone who works where incoming mail is opened. Someplace like an accounts receivable office where payments are still made by mail. Ask that person if it is possible to save the empty envelopes for you if they can.

6

Conclusion

When we are new at something it usually takes time and practice to get good at whatever it is. That, like so many other hobbies, is true where collecting stamps is concerned. You will learn some difficult lessons along the way, so it is always good practice to ask someone before you do something whether that is buying a new stamp, what album to start your collection and even bigger ones like my difficult lesson. In the 1940's Ruby must have known someone who worked at an insurance office receiving incoming mail and payments. That person saved the corners of envelopes with the postmarks and the stamp attached. The box mostly had 3-cent stamps on the pieces of envelope paper. The stamp is a Violet stamp with a large, stylized eagle in the shape of a "V" and was issued on the Fourth of July 1942 in an attempt to bolster American support for the war effort. It is Scott Catalog number 905.

In the 1940's Ruby told me that she would soak the stamps in water and the stamps would easily come off of the paper backing unharmed minus the stamps glue. Soaking stamps will remove stamps from paper and is the correct way to do it. Even today's self-adhesive stamps will soak off their paper backings. Some earlier self-adhesive stamps will not soak off their backing.

CONCLUSION

I was in a hurry to do something with my new to me 50 year-old stamps so into the kitchen sink they went! All of them, about 150 of them with perfect postmarks from all over the country! I was so proud of myself sliding the stamps off the paper and rinsing them in clean cold water and laying them between paper towels to dry. I never gave any thought to how much DNA and germs were in that water that night. When I was finished, I let the water out of the sink, wadded up all the postmarked pieces of paper and threw them away in the trash. What I would do today to have all those stamps and pieces of paper back in the old box waiting to be examined by a new generation soon. Sure, that person will get all of those beautiful stamps, but he or she will not get the history of them. Don't soak your stamps unless you have a reason to do it. By the way, I have a couple boxes of envelope corners that I've accumulated to pass on, so I did learn from my hard-earned lesson.

End of Book Challenge

Find a Stamp Collectors Club or Stamp Show scheduled to meet in your area and make plans to attend the club's next meeting or the stamp show.

Just A Request

I truly do hope that you enjoyed reading this book about stamp collecting and that you consider making it a lifelong hobby. If you have any thoughts about the book, would you please consider leaving a review on the books Amazon review page? It will be a great help for me and thank you for letting me share this book with you. Happy Collecting!

Afterword

Resources

Front cover photo credits; Cottonbro Studio via Pexels, Merve Sabin via Pexels

Back cover photo credit; Jievani via Pexels

Sella, I. (2024, April 19). *Stamps printed - U.S. Postal Facts*. Postal Facts - U.S. Postal Service. https://facts.usps.com/19-billion-stamps-printed/

United States Postal Service - March 29, 2023. (2023, March 29). *Stamps | Postal Facts - U.S. Postal Service*. Postal Facts - U.S. Postal Service. https://facts.usps.com/stamps/

Modern period (1940-Present) | National Postal Museum. (n.d.). https://postalmuseum.si.edu/exhibition/about-us-stamps/modern-period-1940-present

Defining the classic era of stamp collecting - Stamp Community Forum. (n.d.). This Forum Code Is Copyright (C) 2000-05 Michael Anderson, Pierre Gorissen, Huw Reddick and Richard Kinser, Non-Forum Related Code Is Copyright (C) 2007 - 2014 Stamp Community Forums. https://www.stampcommunity.org/topic.asp?TOPIC_ID=56772

Whereabouts unknown for 100 years, Jenny Invert 49 surfaces. (n.d.). Linns Stamp News. https://www.linns.com/news/us-stamps-postal-history/whereabouts-unknown-100-years-jenny-invert.html

Penny Black. (n.d.). Stanley Gibbons. https://www.stanleygibbons.com/shop/great-britain/penny-black

Scott Stamp. (n.d.). Scott Stamp. https://www.scottstamp.com/

MysticStamp. (2024, August 15). *All about watermarks on postage*

AFTERWORD

stamps. Mystic Stamp Learning Center. https://info.mysticstamp.com/learn/watermarks-on-postage-stamps/#:~:text=Watermarks%20were%20introduced%20in%201895,the%20paper%20in%20affected%20areas.

Do you know the important parts of a cover? (n.d.). Linns Stamp News. https://www.linns.com/insights/do-you-know-the-important-parts-of-a-cover-.html

905 - 1942 3C Win the war. (n.d.). Mystic Stamp Company. https://www.mysticstamp.com/905-1942-3c-win-the-war/

Printed in Dunstable, United Kingdom